Piano Accompaniment

Instrumental Solos

Arranged by Bill Galliford, Ethan Neuburg and Tod Edmondson

Produced by
Alfred Music Publishing Co., Inc.
P.O. Box 10003
Van Nuys, CA 91410-0003
alfred.com

Printed in USA.

ISBN-10: 0-7390-7487-3
ISBN-13: 978-0-7390-7487-9

Alfred Cares. Contents printed on 100% recycled paper, except pages 1–4 and 61–64, which are printed on 60% recycled paper.

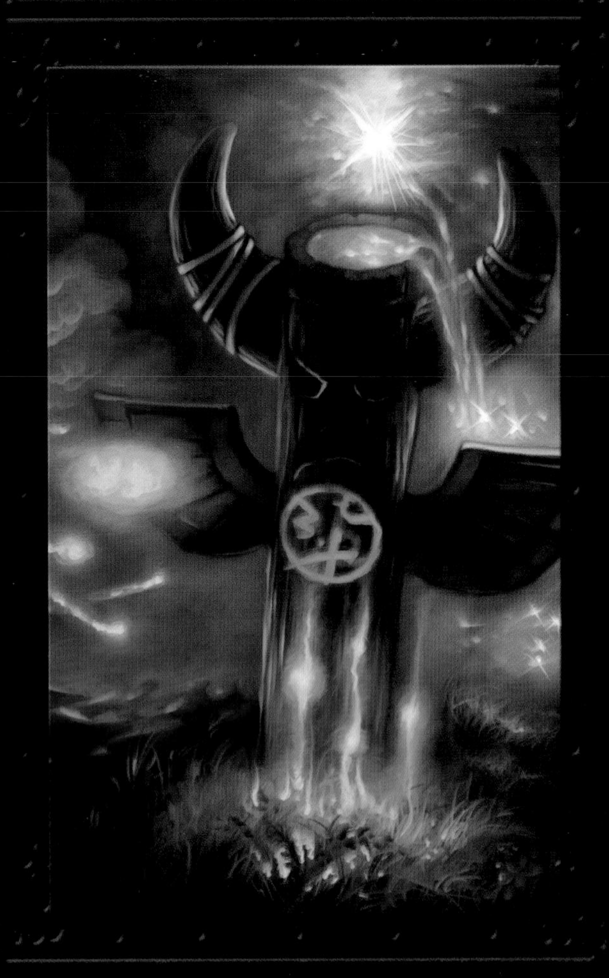

WEI 06

Contents

LION'S PRIDE

Music by
JASON HAYES

Moderately bright ♩ = 182
(𝅗𝅥. = 60 This represents the song pulse counted in one)

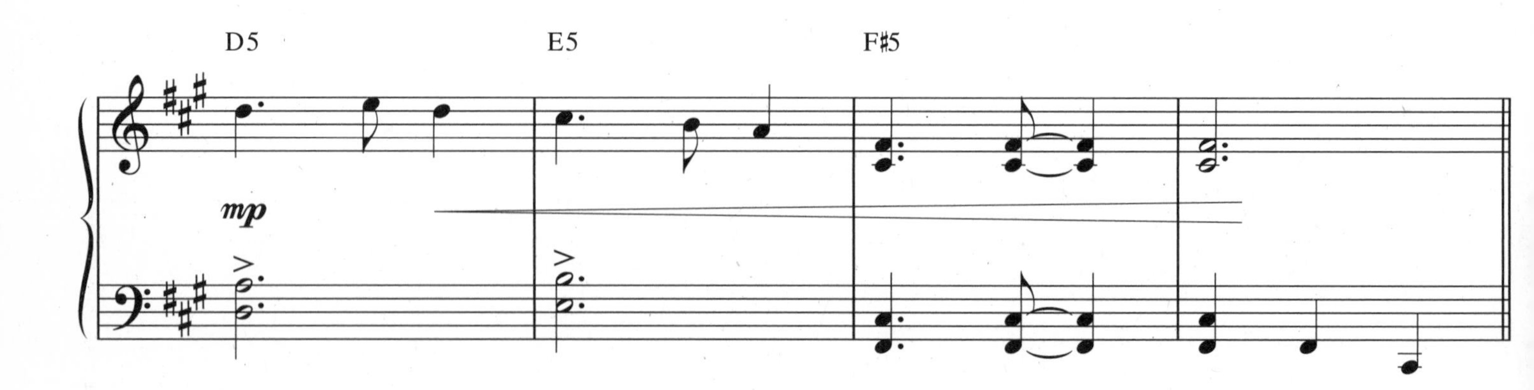

17
D
E
F♯5

33
mf
mf
D5
E
F♯5

49
mp
mp
D5
E
F♯5

65
mf
D5
E5
F♯5
mp

81
C♯5
F♯5
D5
E5
F♯5

97
mf
mf

113
mp
mf
f
f
C♯5
E5
F♯5
ff
ff

THE SHAPING OF THE WORLD

Music by
JASON HAYES

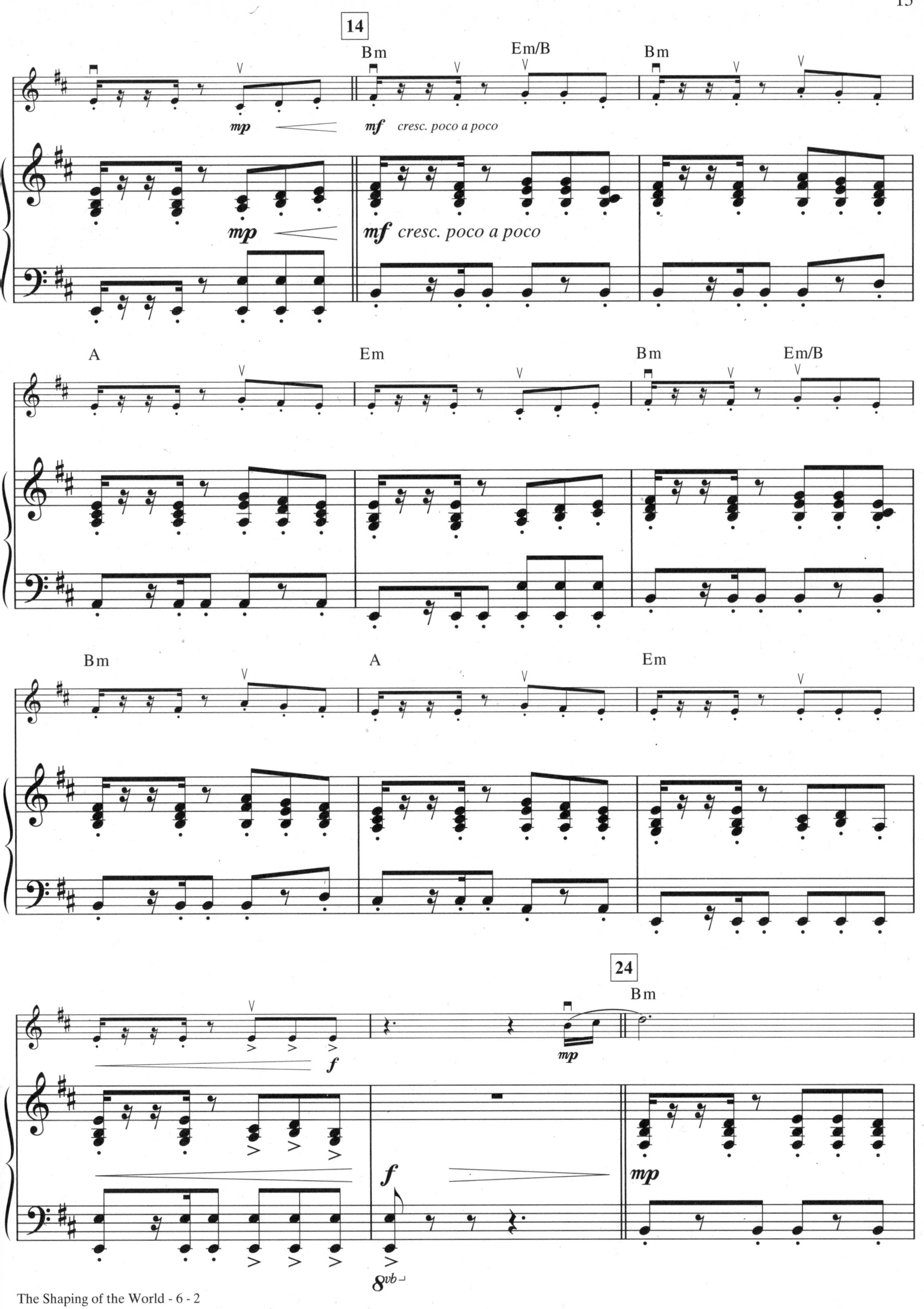
14
Bm
Em/B
Bm
mp
mf
cresc. poco a poco
mp
mf cresc. poco a poco
A
Em
Bm
Em/B
Bm
A
Em
24
Bm
f
mp
f
mp
8vb

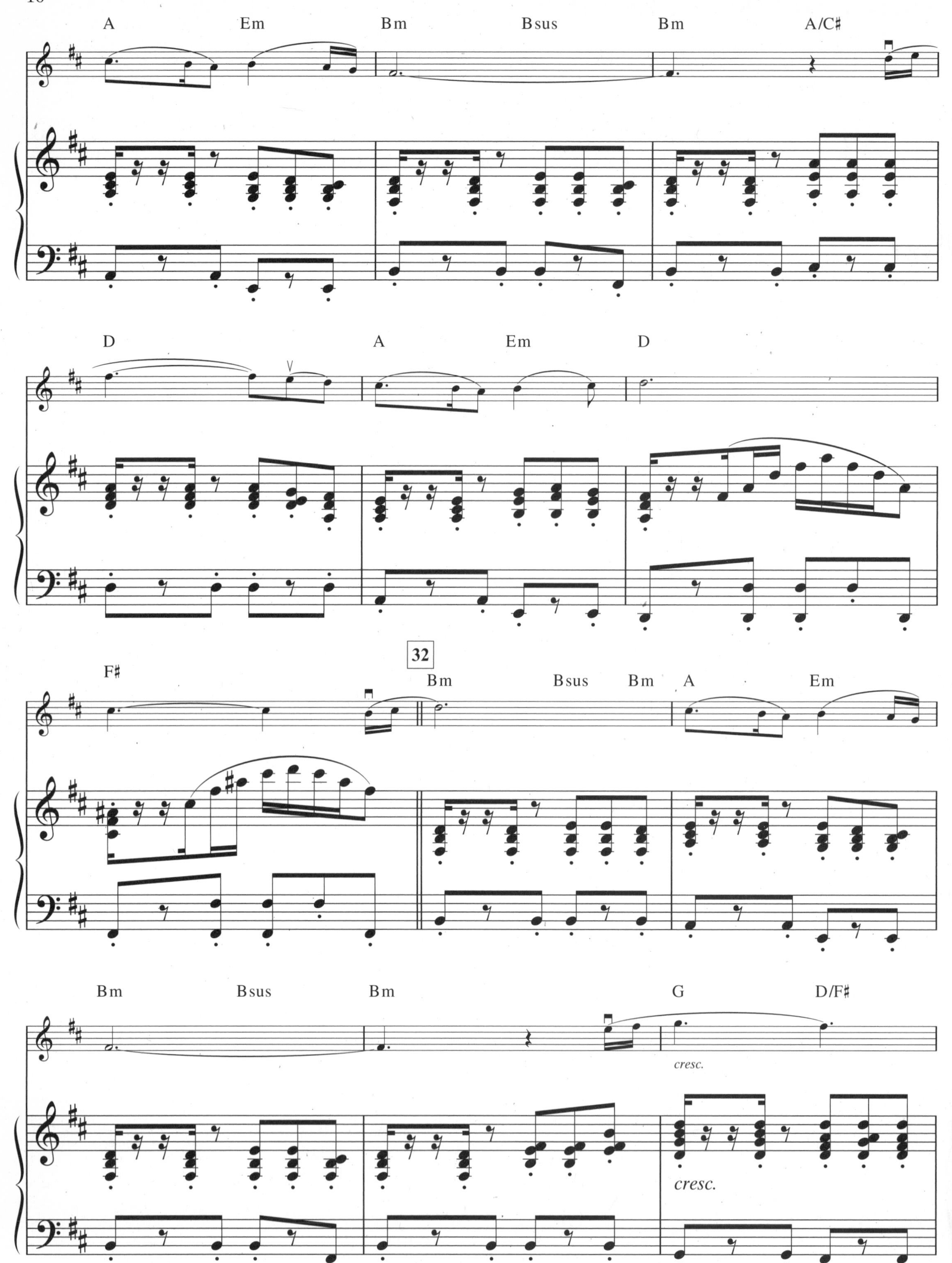
A
Em
Bm
Bsus
Bm
A/C♯
D
A
Em
D
F♯
32
Bm
Bsus
Bm
A
Em
Bm
Bsus
Bm
G
D/F♯
cresc.
cresc.

Em
Bm/D
F♯
Bm/F♯
F♯7
Bm/F♯
mf
cresc. poco a poco
mf
cresc. poco a poco
A7/F♯
D/F♯
Em9/F♯
F♯
F♯m
42
Am
f
f
G
Dm
Am
Asus
Am
G/B
C
G
Dm
C

50
E
Am
G
Dm
Am
Asus
Am
F
C/E
Dm
D♯dim7
E
58
E7
mf
mf

Am
Asus
Am
Asus
mp
Am
66
Asus
Am
mp
decresc. poco a poco
decresc. poco a poco
Asus
Am
Asus
p
p
Am
Asus
Am
pp

SLAUGHTERED LAMB

Music by
DAVID ARKENSTONE

17
Cm
E♭
F
Cm
E♭
F
Cm
E♭
F
E♭
F
B♭
C

33
Dm
C
Dm
mf
mf
C
Dm
C
Dm
C
Dm
C
Dm

49
F
Cm
E♭
F
Cm
E♭
F
57
F
Cm
E♭
F
E♭
F
E♭
F

65
Cm
mp
F
Cm
mp
F
Cm
F
Cm

F
Cm
F
Cm
F
Cm
F
Cm
F
rit.
rit.

PIG AND WHISTLE

Music by
DAVID ARKENSTONE

C
D
G
21
D
G
D
f
f
C
D
A
D
G
D
G
D

C
D
G
37
E5
D5
E5
D5
E5
mf
D5
E5
D5
C5
B5
E5
D5
E5
D5
E5
mf

1.
D5 E5 D5 Am D5
f
2.
D5
54
E5 D5 E5 D5 E5
mf
D5 E5 D5 E5
mf
D5 E5 D5 E5 D5

E5
D5
B5
D5
E5
D5
E5
D5
E5
D5
E5
D5
E5
D5
E5
D5
E5
D5
E5
D5
E5
D5
E5
D5
E5

INVINCIBLE

Music by
RUSSELL BROWER and JASON HAYES

19
Gm
A
Dm
C
mf
mp
mf
Dm
C
Gm/B♭
Dm
Am/C
27
B♭
C
Dm
Dm
C6
Em/B
Dm
C6
Em/B
Dm
C
Gm/D
A

Instrumental Solos

Contents

Arranged by Bill Galliford, Ethan Neuburg and Tod Edmondson

Produced by
Alfred Music Publishing Co., Inc.
P.O. Box 10003
Van Nuys, CA 91410-0003
alfred.com

Printed in USA.

ISBN-10: 0-7390-7487-3
ISBN-13: 978-0-7390-7487-9

LION'S PRIDE

Music by
JASON HAYES

Moderately bright ♩ = 182
(𝅗𝅥. = 60 This represents the song pulse counted in one)

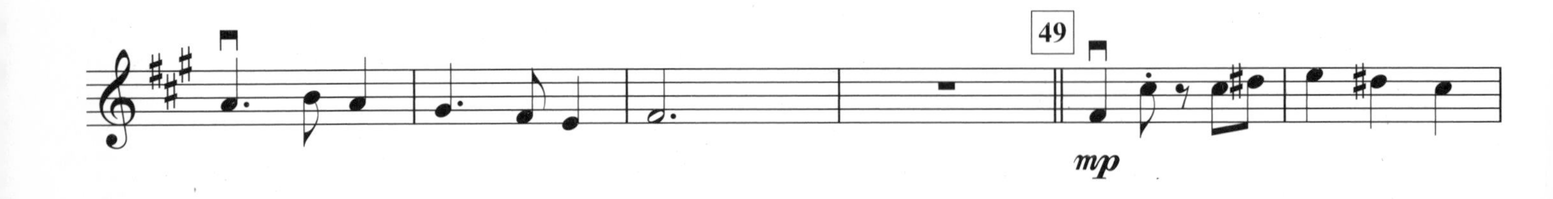

65
16
81
f
97
4
mf
4
113
12
f
ff

THE SHAPING OF THE WORLD

Music by
JASON HAYES

cresc.
mf cresc. poco a poco
(V)
42
f
50
58
mf
5
66
mp
decresc. poco a poco
p

SLAUGHTERED LAMB

Music by
DAVID ARKENSTONE

49
8
57
65
4
mp
3
3
3
rit.

PIG AND WHISTLE

Music by
DAVID ARKENSTONE

37
8
mf
1.
f
2.
54
2
mf
2
2
2

INVINCIBLE

Music by
RUSSELL BROWER and JASON HAYES

A CALL TO ARMS

Music by
JASON HAYES

Track 14: Demo
Track 15: Play Along

WRATH OF THE LICH KING

Music by
RUSSELL BROWER and JASON HAYES

53
Enchanted Forest
legato
f
mf
f
70
March ♩. = 96
Silvermoon 2 Pt. 1
10
mf
ff
f
2
ff
ff
93
Moderately bright ♩ = 130
Silvermoon 2 Pt. 2
2
f
rit. e dim.

Moderately ♩ = 120
Gates of the Black Temple
110
4
f
mp
mf
p
f
rit.
Brighter ♩. = 132
Call to Arms
138
4
f
146
mf
f
cresc. poco a poco
ff
f
Slowly ♩ = 85
Gates of the Black Temple Ending
158
mf
rit.

GATES OF THE BLACK TEMPLE

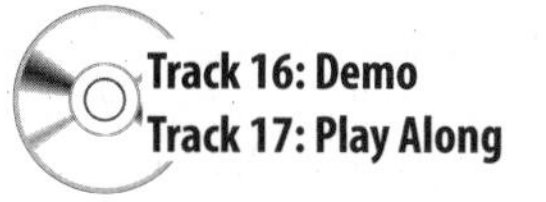

Music by
RUSSELL BROWER

SALTY SAILOR

Music by
DAVID ARKENSTONE

1.
8
2.
8
73

Track 20: Demo
Track 21: Play Along

GARDEN OF LIFE

Music by
RUSSELL BROWER

Instrumental Solos

Lion's Pride

The Shaping of the World

Pig and Whistle

Slaughtered Lamb

Invincible

A Call to Arms

Gates of the Black Temple

Salty Sailor

Wrath of the Lich King

Garden of Life

This book is part of a string series arranged for Violin, Viola, and Cello. The arrangements are completely compatible with each other and can be played together or as solos. Each book features a specially designed piano accompaniment that can be easily played by a teacher or intermediate piano student, as well as a carefully crafted removable part, complete with bowings, articulations and keys well suited for the Level 2-3 player. A fully orchestrated accompaniment CD is also provided. The CD includes a DEMO track of each song, which features a live string performance, followed by a PLAY-ALONG track.

This book is also part of Alfred's World of Warcraft Instrumental Solos series written for Flute, Clarinet, Alto Sax, Tenor Sax, Trumpet, Horn in F and Trombone. An orchestrated accompaniment CD is included. A **piano accompaniment** book (optional) is also available. Due to level considerations regarding keys and instrument ranges, the arrangements in the **wind instrument** series are not compatible with those in the **string instrument** series.

World of Warcraft • Instrumental Solos • Violin

Alfred

alfred.com

Dm
C
Em/B
A
Em
Am/E
D
D7
Bm
A
A+
A
Gm
A
41
Dm
C
Dm
C
Gm/B♭
Dm
Am/C
B♭
C
Dm
molto rit.
molto rit.

A CALL TO ARMS

Music by
JASON HAYES

Moderately slow ♩ = 84

Quickly, boldly ♩. = 132
14
f
f
sim.
ff
f
22
mf
mf

cresc.
f
cresc. poco a poco
30
ff
f
Tempo I ♩ = 84
mf
rit. e dim.
mp
8vb

WRATH OF THE LICH KING

Music by
RUSSELL BROWER and JASON HAYES

March ♩ = 160

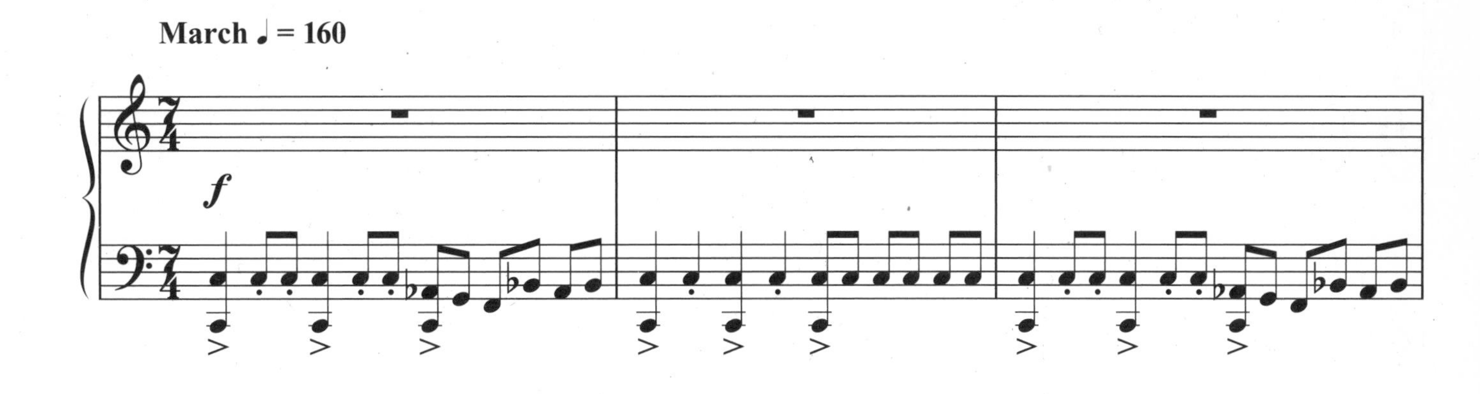

Slowly ♩ = 66
32 Northrend One
mf
mp
mf

36
f
f
ff
ff
mf
mf
7
7
f

mf
f
mf
53 Enchanted Forest
legato
f
mf
f

mf
March ♩. = 96
70 Silvermoon 2 Pt. 1
f

mf
mf
ff
f
ff
f
(𝅗𝅥 = 𝅘𝅥.)
ff
ff
ff
ff

*F♭ = E♮

rit. e dim.
rit. e dim.
Moderately ♩ = 120
110 Gates of the Black Temple
mf

f
f
mp
mp
mf
mf
p
p
8vb
8vb

f
f
rit.
rit.
Brighter ♩. = 132
138
Call to Arms
f
sim.

ff
f
f
146
mf
mf
cresc.
f
f
cresc. poco a poco
cresc. poco a poco

ff
f
Slowly ♩ = 85
158 Gates of the Black Temple Ending
mf
rit.
p
8vb

GATES OF THE BLACK TEMPLE

Music by
RUSSELL BROWER

17
Dm
p
p
25
B♭/D
Dm
G
f
f
Dm
B♭/D
Dm
G
rit.
rit.

SALTY SAILOR

Music by
DAVID ARKENSTONE

G
A5
D
A5
G
A5
F
G
A5
25
G
A5
Em
A5
G
A5
F
G
A5

G
A5
D
A5
G
A5
F
G
A5
41
G
Am
G
A5
G
C
F
G

Am
G
A5
F5
C/F
G
F
E5
1.
A5
G6
A5
E5
2.
A5
G5
A5
E5

A5
G5
A5
F5
G5
A5
73
G5
A5
D5
A5
G5
A5
F5
G5
A5
Am
G
A5
E5

Am
G
A5
F
G
A5
G
A5
D5
A5
G
A5
F
G
Am
F5
G5
A5
F5
G5
A5

GARDEN OF LIFE

Music by
RUSSELL BROWER

17
25
mf
mf

33
41
f
f

49
mp
mp
57
p
molto rit.